Invest in Australian and US Stock Market and Make Money

A practical guide on investing for international students, temporary residents, and citizens in Australia

By

Gayleg Zangmo

Copyright © 2025 Gayleg Zangmo

All of the information in this book is based on my own experiences and personal opinions related to stock market investing. I am not a qualified financial expert, advisor or analyst. The material shared here is only to be used for general information and educational purposes and is not intended to be taken as professional financial advice. We strongly recommend that readers carry out their own research or consult with a qualified financial advisor before making any investments.

Dedication

Dedicated to my late father who introduced the world of investing to me.

Acknowledgement

I would like to thank my mom who is the most kind-hearted person in the world. She worked hard to bring us up and who also gave us the wings of independence and roots of responsibility.

I would like to thank my late father who believed that education is the greatest investment in life and left no stone unturned to educate all five children in any ways possible.

My thanks will also go to my childhood friends, school friends, college friends and university colleagues and work colleagues who provided support and assistance throughout my life and making who I am today.

Thank you to all teachers in my life who has supported me during my studies and also to my work supervisors who provided support and assistance in my professional life.

Table Of Contents

Chapter 1:
Why You Should Invest:
Building Financial Independence

For many people who migrate to Australia, whether it be for studying, working, or starting a new life, money often seems like a constant stress. Given the combination of rent, tuition fees, and day-to-day living expenses, you would be pleased if you saved anything at all.

Here is the hidden truth: saving alone is not enough. In a land of quietly rising inflation over every year, the money you have sitting in your account right now will buy you less in the future. You may think you are being responsible by 'keeping your money safe' in the bank; believe me, your money in the bank is losing value day-by-day.

In a 2023 report from ASIC, only a little less than one in three Australians aged between 18–29 years invest in the share market[1]. This number is even lower if you are an international student or temporary resident. By comparison, the annual average inflation is around 4%, meaning money sitting in your savings account earning 1–2% interest rates is essentially losing purchasing power every year[2].

Take a young woman named Mei who is a 25-year-old international student from Malaysia. She worked part-time at a café and was able to save around A$5,000 over her two-year course work. When she checked her balance after graduation, she was gleaming with pride; until she realised that the rising rent, groceries, and living costs had climbed nearly 10% since she arrived. Her savings had not grown; they had *shrunk in value*.

---

[1] Australian Securities and Investments Commission (ASIC). *Young Australians and Investing*, 2023.

[2] Reserve Bank of Australia. *Measures of Consumer Price Inflation*, September 2025.

Then there is Samir, a temporary resident who thought investing was only for rich people. He was scared of investing and said, 'I will just lose everything.' After being in Australia for five years, his savings account made him less than 2% of interest returns and inflation averaged around 4%. Basically, he lost money without doing anything.

These are not isolated cases. These cases reflect a general challenge faced by young adults, students, and even working professionals alike - fear, confusion, and knowledge gaps around investing.

According to a 2023 report from the Australia Security and Investments Commission (ASIC), only about one in three young Australians aged 18-29 actively invest in the stock market. Even lower for international students and new residents.

Meanwhile, in recent years inflation in Australia has been around 3-5% a year on average and most savings accounts earn less than 2%. This means your money is quietly being weakened the longer it has no assigned purpose.

The gap of what people earn versus what their money could earn generally keeps people engaged in a loop of: work, save, spend and repeat. The greatest threat is not necessarily losing financially in the market, it is also losing time. Every year you postpone investing signifies one more year of possible expansion you could be losing. Compounding (the process of earning a return on your return) can only motivate early starters who engage in the habit.

By not investing, people regularly forfeit the possibility of allowing their cash to work for them in order to purchase a home earlier, travel without a ton of debt, or simply stop stressing about every single penny.

This book is for anyone who has ever told themselves, 'Investing sounds too complicated for me' or 'I will start in when I have more dollars.' It is for students, new residents, and common people who want to take control of their financial future without studying finance or having thousands of dollars to start.

You will be able to start small, gradually grow, and eventually get to genuine financial independence with manageable action steps and important strategies through real world examples.

The aim is not to get rich quick. It is to allow you to get to a point where your money stealthily grows in the background, resulting in more time, more freedom and more mental peace to live the life you intended on when you first arrived in Australia.

In reality, the common argument is that people struggle not because of a lack of money, they simply struggle because their money is not growing. After you learn how inflation silently eats away at savings and how speculation often stops people from taking the next step, it is time to move on from the problem to the solution. The solution is learning how to have your money work for you. This starts with investing, not as a risky toss of the dice but as a practical, established way to achieve long-term financial independence.

When it comes to money, it is safe to say that for most of their childhood, people heard, 'save what you earn, do not take risks around money.' While this might have worked for some years ago, today it is simply not enough in the modern economy. Prices go up every year, salaries are often not increasing, and the cost of living in Australia is going up faster than most savings.

Why Investing Matters

Inflation, the slow rise in prices over time, quietly decreases the purchasing power of your money. In Australia, inflation has been on average 3–5% over the last few years. That means if you leave A$10,000 in a savings account earning an interest rate of 2% per year, you would effectively be losing approximately 1–3% of the real value of your money each year. You may not see it for a few years, but the reduction in purchasing power certainly adds up after 10 years.

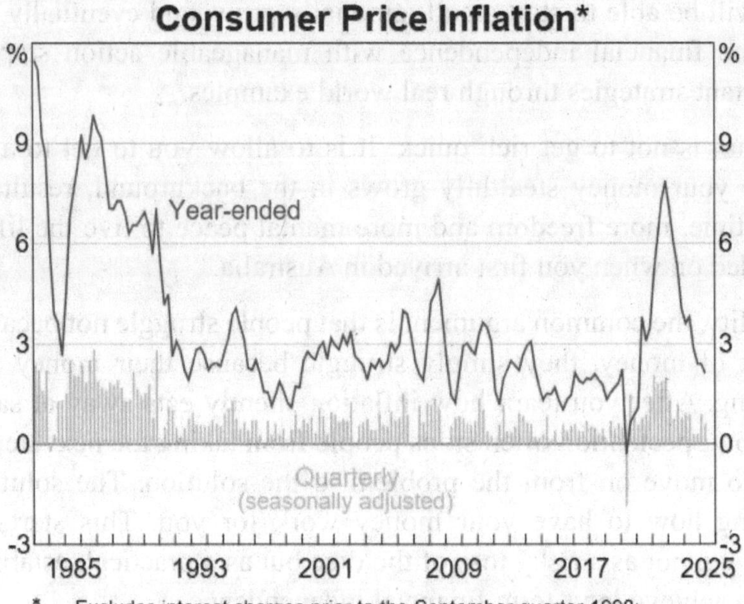

Reserve Bank of Australia, 'Measures of Consumer Price Inflation' Sept 2025.

This is where investing plays an important role. Investing allows your money to grow at a greater rate than inflation can erode it. Investing is not about *pick your stock that will outpace the market* or gamble, it is about recognising that money can earn money on top of money, simply through compounding returns. Compounding occurs when your investment gains themselves begin to generate money. This creates an exponential effect, and over time you will really be earning money.

Over the last 30 years, the Australian share market (ASX 200) has returned an average of approximately 8% each year while banks and savings accounts can only offer up to 2% at best; this difference can really compound over a long period of time[3].

Think of a newly planted tree. During its first year of growth, it is small and vulnerable. As it continues to develop, that tree gains strength and begins to produce fruit. The fruit it produces contains seeds that can

---

[3] ASX. *Long-Term Market Performance Data*, 2024.

produce new trees. This is how compounding works. With a small, consistent commitment you can see exponential growth over time.

For example, if you invested just A$100 each month into an ETF that earned an average of 8% per year, after ten years you would have A$18,000. If you had simply saved the same money, you would have A$12,000 in a bank earning 2%. The difference of A$6,000 is compounding at work[4].

Remember Aisha, a 27-year-old international student living in Sydney? When Aisha heard of investing for the first time, she was uncertain. She thought of investing as something for someone with lots of money or a finance degree. But, after some research, she was able to make an investment commitment of starting with A$20 a week and using beginner-friendly apps like Spaceship Voyager and CommSec Pocket.

She decided to keep it simple and use a portfolio of ETFs that tracked the overall Australian and US markets. She did not check her balance every day or worry about dips in the market. She faced the markets with discipline and consistency!

When we met again three years later, she shared with me that her small weekly contributions had grown to more than A$4,000, of which she had invested about A$3,100 and the rest was from returns. This is when she realised that investing was less about market timing or getting rich quick, and more about patience, education and consistency.

Her story demonstrates that it is not about being rich enough to invest; you get rich by starting earlier and developing your discipline.

---

[4] Moneysmart.gov.au. *Compound Interest Calculator Example*, 2025

Shares, ETFs, and Dividends, The Building Blocks

Let us simplify what you can invest in locally.

1. Shares

A share simply means ownership in a small piece of a company. For example:

- When you buy Woolworths shares, you own part of Australia's largest supermarket.
- When you buy Commonwealth Bank shares, you own part of one of the strongest banks in the Southern Hemisphere.

If the company generates a profit, you might receive dividends as a shareholder, which are regular cash payments in general every six months.

2. ETFs (Exchange-Traded Funds)

An ETF represents a collection of shares grouped together. Rather than purchasing into just one company, you purchase dozens or even hundreds of shares of multiple companies at once. For a beginner, this is usually the smartest way to start as it is simple, cheap and diversified.

For example: 'Vanguard Australian Shares ETF (VAS)' is an investment into the top 300 companies on the Australian Stock Exchange (ASX) all at once. This means you own a small piece of the total Australian economy all in one go.

3. Dividends, The Passive Income Power

Australia is known for something called franked dividends. That means the tax already paid by the company is credited to you and reduced from your own tax bill. This is one of the most valuable things about being an investor in Australia.

According to an S&P Global report for 2024, Australian companies that pay dividends have provided a total return of 9-10% annually, on average, over the last 10-years, including reinvested dividends. This is well above the return on most savings accounts or term deposits.

Mia is a 25-year-old student living in Melbourne who decided to invest using CommSec Pocket app after reading that inflation meant your savings would lose value. She started with only A$50 each month in a *Sustainable Leaders* ETF, which is companies focused on the environment.

After two years, her cumulative contributions were A$1,200. The worth of her investment portfolio is A$1,420. Not an unimaginable amount, but the increase of A$220 (along with some dividends) represented more than numbers; it represented proof she could create wealth herself.

In response to the question of what had changed for her, she said, 'The first time I saw a dividend go into my account - although it was only a handful of dollars, I realised that I was earning money without earning money. That is when I realised what financial independence actually felt like.'

This is the beauty of starting small and being consistent

Stock Market vs. Real Estate

Many individuals think that real estate is the only 'real' product. And yes, real estate can be a great asset but it is not possible for everyone to access. Even purchasing a small apartment in Sydney requires tens of thousands of dollars in advance, not to mention ongoing mortgage repayments, property tax, and expenses associated with maintaining a property.

As of 2024, the average NSW house price is over A$1.1million - so you will require at least an A$220,000 deposit! In comparison, it is possible for anyone to invest in an ETF through an app such as CommSec Pocket app for as little as A$50!

So, in that sense, the stock market provides you with the possibility to start small and stay flexible. For stocks, you can invest a minimum of A$5- A$10 using apps like Spaceship Voyager or CommSec Pocket app and then slowly raise your contributions as your income grows.

Real estate could be considered illiquid - there is no way to sell off a part of the house to acquire cash if necessary. With stocks you can sell some or all of your stock with one-click or a few clicks on your phone. This flexibility makes investing in stock much more practical for students, new residents, and everyone who is building wealth on a budget.

Think of it this way: both property and shares can help you grow wealth, but the stock market is the most accessible and scalable place to start. It gives you a way to participate in the growth of the world's biggest companies, from Apple to Woolworths, without needing millions in capital.

Not a Pyramid Scheme, A Regulated Market

Consider it this way: both property and shares can provide a means of growing wealth, but the stock market is the most straightforward and scalable place to start. It can offer you direct exposure to the growth of the world's largest companies, from Apple to Woolworths, without needing millions to invest.

One common fear beginning investors have is, 'What if I lose everything? What if this is a scam?' These fears are perfectly rational, particularly in a digital world that is saturated with online trading 'experts', social media influencers who proclaim profits in hours, and apps that disappear overnight with your money.

Before you invest a single dollar, it is crucial to breakdown the difference between legitimate investing and pyramid schemes or scams.

Pyramid scheme is a fraudulent business model that relies on the willingness of participants to recruit people into a business opportunity instead of selling real products or services. Early scheme participants are paid bi-weekly with the money from newer recruits into the concept. The scheme promotes upselling products, mentioning high returns for less risk, both of which should be a red flag.

Pyramid schemes are specifically prohibited by the Australian Consumer Law (ACL) in Australia. The Australian Competition and Consumer Commission (ACCC) specifically notes that any situation where the income is primarily generated from enrolling others - rather than the sale of actual products or services - is considered a pyramid scheme.

There are serious legal outcomes if you participate in, advertise or assist someone in enrolling in a pyramid scheme, including criminal prosecution and potential fines of up to A$220,000 for individuals and A$1.1 million for corporations. In addition to these fines, there is the potential to have your financial record and credibility tarnished. It is best practice to always check that any investment opportunity involves investment activities that are regulated by an Australian authority, such as the Australian Securities and Investments Commission (ASIC) or the Australian Securities Exchange (ASX), and not placing your money into an unregulated scheme.

Here is how it typically works:

- You are invited to 'invest' or 'join a program'. You are told that you will earn a percentage of the money from every person you bring in.

- The structure keeps growing like a pyramid, wide at the bottom, narrow at the top.

- Eventually, when new members stop joining, the money dries up, and the entire structure collapses.

Most individuals experience financial losses, while only a small group at the top is actually profiting. There is no genuine business, no actual product, and no realistic basis for everyone to win.

In contrast, the stock market, although having some basic similarities with a marketing scheme, is entirely different. Joining and recruiting others are not part of the equation - you are investing in ownership.

When you purchase a share of a stock, whether that stock is Woolworths, Common-wealth Bank, or Apple, you are buying a piece of that business. By investing, you are entitled to a portion of the profit generated by the company through dividends and drive growth through price appreciation.

Companies listed on the Australian Securities Exchange (ASX) are real businesses that provide goods and services, employ people, pay taxes and contribute positively to the economy. While the value of your investment is dependent on their performance, your success is not reliant on recruiting new investors after you into the scheme as there might be regarding a multi-level marketer.

This is what separates a regulated market from a manipulative scheme.

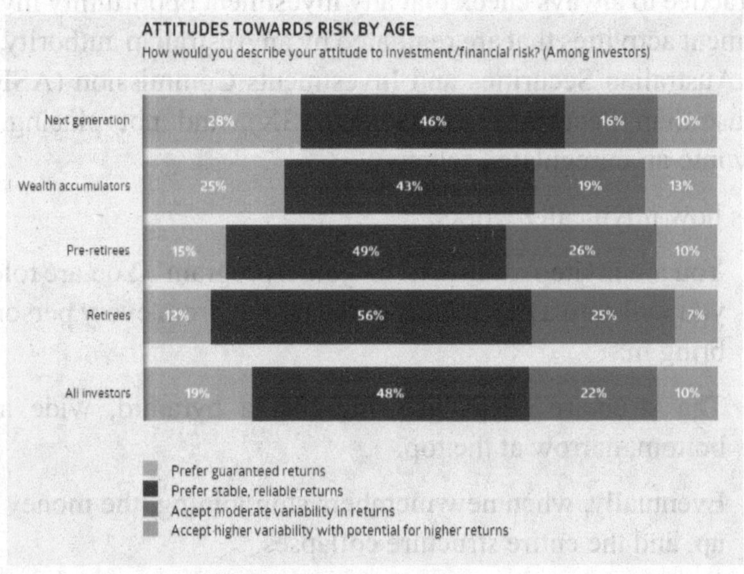

Attitudes towards investment/financial risk by age group. The Role of ASIC and Regulation

People's perceptions of risk evolve with time. Younger investors, referred to as 'Next generation' are more willing to accept greater variability with the possibility of higher returns, as the graph above illustrates, whereas older, retired investors are more inclined toward 'stable and reliable returns.' This mentality change is crucial because, if you acknowledge that you are younger, you may have more time and, consequently, more capacity to accept moderate risk. This is the first step toward expanding your portfolio rather than protecting capital.

The Australian Securities and Investments Commission (ASIC) is the governmental agency charged with regulating financial markets, protecting investors and enforcing the law. ASIC provides assurance that any company or financial service operating in Australia adheres to rigorous standards of transparency and accountability.

Every company on the ASX is mandated to:

- Publish audited financial statements at least biannually.
- Disclose any material information (such as profit, risk, or change in management) to the public immediately.
- Comply with rules of corporate governance, which prevent manipulation and insider trading.
- Incur penalties or even suspension, if they mislead investors.

In other words, you don't have to 'trust' someone's word, you can seek and verify the information directly through routinely available reports and information. That is how a regulated market works, and it is based upon disclosure rather than dependency.

Why the Fear Exists and Why It is Misplaced

Many people, especially new investors, often confuse investing with a scam, as this is what they see on social media advertising. They see remarks like 'double your money in 10 days' or 'guaranteed monthly income.' Those are flags of a scheme - not investing. Trustworthy investment in the stock market does not promise where you get the money in an instant. Rather, honest investing rewards patience, education, development, and consistency. Although prices rise and fall (and risk always exists), you can invest in an environment that is transparent, legal, and heavily regulated, where a company has to behave *fairly*.

When a public company does not provide material information or takes liberties with the facts, ASIC can issue penalties, launch inquiries and ultimately delist that company from the ASX. This has occurred several times within the past decade demonstrating that regulation is not simply a discussion point; it is something the state implements on your behalf.

In stark contrast, when a pyramid scheme fails, there is often no regulator, no transparency, and no recovery from loss as it was never legal to begin with. The Distinction is Important.

Here is the distinction:

- Pyramid schemes are based on recruitment and secrecy with unrealistic and unsustainable promises.
- The stock market is based on regulation and transparency with the real prospect of economic growth.

When you invest using registered platforms like CommSec Pocket app, Spaceship Voyager, or SelfWealth in the ASX or global markets you are investing into one of the most well in-regulated and law-governed financial systems in the world.

This lowers you from fear to confidence. You are not just *joining a system;* you are becoming an owner in real businesses investing in the global economy. You are not waiting for others to join after you, and you are investing on productivity, innovation and the global economy.

That is not gambling, that is smart investing in a reasonable trusting regulated marketplace.

The Mindset for Financial Freedom

Financial freedom does not mean being a millionaire. It means having enough passive income – income generated from your investments – that you can pay your bills without having to rely on an employer for a paycheck or borrow from others.

Achieving this requires three things: discipline, patience and education.

- Discipline means making regular contributions regardless of how much you can contribute.
- Patience means staying invested in the market no matter the ups and downs, knowing time will smooth out the volatility.
- Education means learning what it means to manage risk, diversification, and how investments align with your purpose.

Studies done by Vanguard have shown that investors who stay invested for at least ten years earn an average of double the returns compared to investors who buy and sell frequently. It is consistency - not timing - that makes you a successful investor.

Just remember, building wealth is not about luck - it is about habit. The sooner you begin, the longer your money has time to compound and the more freedom you will gain later in life.

As you will see in the next chapters, investing is not just for 'the rich' or 'the financial elite'. It is a skill you can learn, practice, and develop like any other skill. Using the right mindset, tools and knowledge you can drastically change the trajectory of your financial future - one small habitual and consistent investment at a time.

You can choose to be financially independent. Your money can begin to work for you today and every dollar in a growth asset takes you one step closer to that freedom.

Self-Reflection Questions

1. Is fear or not feeling smart enough keeping me from growing my money?
2. If I decided my only activity was to save and not invest, what might my financial life look like in 10 years?
3. What does financial independence mean to me personally?
4. What is my timeline of when I will take my first, small step and start investing?

Chapter 2:
Getting Started:
Your First Steps into the Stock Market

Having learned that investing is crucial for financial independence, it is now time to take your first step in the market. Most individuals never get past this level. They may acknowledge that investment is crucial, but they never even get started. This chapter will seek to change that inactivity into action. Beginning can be daunting.

You might believe you need thousands of dollars or extensive financial experience before you can invest. But the reality is that you can start with as little as A$50. There are apps such as CommSec Pocket and Spaceship Voyager for precisely this reason. They enable beginners to invest with ease. You only have to download an app and select a theme or ETF that suits your purpose.

In the 2024 HSBC survey, one in four (26%) Australians still only occasionally invest. Regular investors will always beat sporadic investors in the long run, as well as in overall confidence[5]. Those who choose automatic, routine investments (even tiny ones) are most likely to see them through bull and bear markets and to collect consistent returns.

Now let us place 'waiting' in context. If you save A$50 a week at an interest rate of 7% a year for ten years, you will have about A$37,000. But if you keep waiting three years and invest the same amount, you will get approximately $A26, 000 instead, simply because you waited three years too long. That is more than an A$11, 000 difference simply because one opted to do it later.

This is referred to as the 'cost of waiting', and it is one of the most undervalued losses in personal finance. Time is the most potent

---

[5] HSBC. *Australian Investor Insights Report*, 2024.

element of investing, and the sooner you begin, the less work you will have to do in the future.

The table below, based on Moneysmart data, shows how investing small amounts regularly can accumulate into substantial wealth over a decade, simply through discipline and compounding[6].

Fortnightly contributions amount	Balance after 10 years
$200	$72,834
$250	$90,587
$300	$108,341
$350	$126,095
$400	$143,848
$450	$161,602

How incremental investing can add up over 10 years | Moneysmart.gov.au

Investing is not forecasting the market; it is participating in the market. Even the most experienced investors do not know precisely when the market will peak or trough, so consistency has to be your best friend.

According to the 2025 report by Macquarie Asset Management, the average one-year return following a market peak was 9.8%. This is evidence that remaining invested during times of volatility yields higher returns than trying to time the peaks and troughs.

Do not worry about waiting for the 'right moment'; instead, incorporate regular savings into your daily routine of investing, similarly like paying bills or shopping for groceries.

Let us consider what Australian generations are already investing in before going into the details of how to start. Small and frequent investing is taking over, and the habits of Gen Z, Millennials, and other investors reflect the changing financial mindsets.

---

[6] Moneysmart.gov.au. *Regular Investing Growth Scenarios*, 2025.

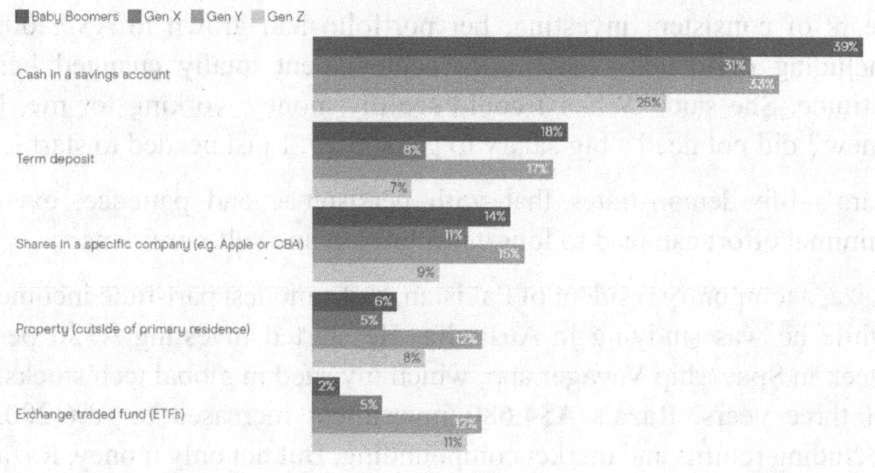

Investment product ownership by generation in Australia. Finder. (2024) [7].

Simple Tools to Get You Started

1. CommSec Pocket

CommSec Pocket lets you invest in themed ETFs starting from A$50. This is perfect for beginners who want to learn how the Australian Securities Exchange (ASX) works.

2. Spaceship Voyager

Spaceship Voyager lets you invest just A$5 in portfolios featuring Australian and US companies such as Apple, Google, and CSL. This is a simple app that automatically reinvests, keeping your portfolio growing with little effort. Both apps are ASIC-regulated, so you can be confident that your money is in good hands with solid providers and is kept securely and openly.

Sara, 22, an international student in Sydney, thought she needed thousands before investing. But when she heard about CommSec Pocket app, she invested A$50 per week into an Australian ETF. Her portfolio was initially small, only a few hundred dollars. After two

---

[7] Finder Australia. *Investment Statistics and Trends 2024.*

years of consistent investing, her portfolio had grown to A$2,200, including dividends. That minor achievement totally changed her attitude. She said, 'When I could see my money working for me, I knew I did not need a big salary to get started; I just needed to start.'

Sara's life demonstrates that with persistence and patience, even minimal effort can lead to long-term growth and self-confidence.

Raza, a temporary resident of Pakistan, had a modest part-time income while he was studying in Australia. He started investing A$30 per week in Spaceship Voyager app, which invested in global tech stocks. In three years, Raza's A$4,680 investment increased to A$6,200, including returns and market compounding. But not only money, Raza also attained knowledge, discipline, and confidence in his financial future. He added, 'Even when markets declined, I did not cease investing. I knew my actual return was in developing a habit.'

More Popular Investment Apps

1. Raiz

Raiz allows you to invest the spare change from your everyday purchases by rounding them up to the nearest dollar and investing the left-over amount for you. With a minimum starting amount of around A$5, Raiz is an excuse-free way to start investing and building good habits for any beginners who may need an ease in automated contributions. This app can be used by only Australian citizens.

2. InvestSMART

InvestSMART is a bit more of a research platform and investment-management portal. It provides access to professional insights, portfolio tracking, and managed funds. InvestSMART is great for investment-focused people who value a more analytical side of investing and support to help inform any decisions.

3. SelfWealth

SelfWealth has a flat brokerage fee (around $9.50 per US or Australian share trade). It is perfect for anyone who wants to have their own full control over managing investments or trading in general. SelfWealth has CHESS-sponsored ownership of your shares – so they are held directly in your name. This app can be used by only Australian citizens.

4. Moomoo

Moomoo is a global trading platform that allows traders to access Australian, US, Hong Kong, and Chinese markets. It is aimed at investors who want live market data, sophisticated charting tools, and analytics worthy of professionals, without having to pay very high fees. Moomoo is especially appealing to actively trading investors because of its research tools, technical indicators and low brokerage costs on global shares. Moomoo is very easy to use but likely more interesting for someone who enjoys engaging deeper into analyzing and trading than someone who is more passive. Anyone residing in Australia can invest using this app.

5. CMC Markets Invest

CMC Markets Invest, previously CMC Stockbroking, provides access to Australian shares and international shares with brokerage fees lowers as your trading becomes more active. CMC Markets Invest contains excellent research tools, market depth data, and excellent charting features — making it a strong option for active investors wanting to qualify their decisions with a decent amount of backup. CMC Markets Invest offers CHESS sponsored shares for trades on the ASX, which gives you true ownership. CMC Markets Invest is best for intermediate to advanced, active investors who want a professional platform, but also want lower fees.

6. Sharesies

It enables fractional investing by letting you purchase small parts of shares in companies from Australia, the US, and New Zealand. It has no minimum investment to start, making it very beginner-friendly. The app has a bright and cheery design to put you at ease while you invest, making it look straightforward. This would be a useful tool for younger or first-time investors hoping to build a diversified investment portfolio gradually without needing much leverage.

Regular vs. Irregular Investors

Research conducted by HSBC (2025) found that frequent investors who white-labelled their transfers have 40% higher confidence in achieving their capital targets than infrequent investors.

Dollar-cost averaging involves opening a position and accumulating at various prices. An automatic investing habit eliminates the need to make decisions based on what is happening today. 'Time in the market' gives time to compound interest to work over the years. Irregular investors tend to fall prey to emotional investing, buying high and selling low due to fear.

Avoiding Common Beginner Mistakes

- Trying to get rich quickly: The stock market is not a lottery.
- Checking your portfolio every day: This leads to panic.
- Investing in what you do not understand: Always do your research or start with ETFs.
- Ignoring fees and taxes: Know your platform fees and the tax implications.
- Comparing yourself to others in financial matters: Everyone's investment journey is different.

Successful beginner investors focus on education and discipline, not luck and perfect timing.

From Fear to Confidence

The majority of prospective investors are apprehensive since they do not want to lose money. But investing is not gambling; it is about being shareholder/investor in companies or business. Your cash is buying shares in real companies that produce real products and services. You are acquiring an interest in their success. Investing in a regulated financial market, such as Australian stock market, is a smart move because novice investors are protected by laws overseen by ASIC, which promote fairness and accountability.

Your 30-Day Starter Plan

Week	Action	Description
1	Download and explore an investing app	Compare CommSec Pocket, Spaceship Voyager and other investing apps.
2	Set your goal	Decide how much and how often you will invest.
3	Start your first investment	Begin with $20–$50. Do not overthink it.
4	Track and reflect	See how it feels. Focus on building the habit.

You have only just made your first quantifiable step towards financial freedom. You did not arrive there by sipping from a fire hose and waking up richer overnight. Instead, you started by building the habits that get you there.

The secret to starting is that it does not start with money, but with momentum. All those little things actually do count. The sooner you move, the sooner you will thank yourself.

And as the maxim goes, 'The best time to plant a tree is 20 years ago; the second-best time is now.'

So go ahead and open an investing app, do your research, select your initial ETF, and begin investing in yourself, baby steps at a time.

Finally, in Chapter 3, you will find out how to assemble your portfolio in Australia. You will learn how to approach dividend thinking and avoid common newbie mistakes while building a strong base for your Australian investments.

Self-Reflection Questions

1. What is motivating me to invest right now?
2. What am I willing to invest consistently without concern about losing short-term gains?
3. Do I have a clear understanding of saving, gambling, and investing?
4. What would be one small, actionable step to take this week to continue my investment journey?

Chapter 3:
Investing in the Australian Market: Building a Local Portfolio

At this point, you know why you should be investing and how to make your first small investment.

Next, we are going to dig deeper, into your own backyard, the Australian market.

If you live, study, or work in Australia, this market is not just a financial opportunity, it is your local gateway to building real wealth. You see the companies everyday - Woolworths, Coles, Commonwealth Bank, Qantas. They are all around you, and the great thing is you can own them.

This chapter will take you through how the ASX works, how to use beginner-friendly app like ComSec Pocket, and how to build a tax-smart, confident portfolio, step-by-step.

We will also share real stories of some investors who started small and created a base towards financial independence, one share at a time.

Understanding the ASX – Australia's Financial Pulse

The Australian Securities Exchange (ASX) is one of the oldest and most trusted markets globally, companies list their shares on this market and investors like you can buy ownership in this company.

By purchasing shares, you are not betting on a set of random outcomes - you are actually buying into a real business that sells real products to real customers and earns real profits. Each time Woolworths sells groceries or Qantas flies passengers around the world, a proportion of those profits, called dividends, could come back to you as a shareholder.

The ASX 2023 Investor Study found that more than 7.7 million Australians, or roughly 43% of the adult population in Australia, invest in shares or ETFs[8]. Many of these investors started off small, often less than A\$2,000. The study also found that investors who keep their investments for five years or longer were much more likely to get positive returns than traders.

That is a valuable lesson right there - you do not have to predict the market; just invest and be consistent.

Creating an Emergency Fund - Your Safety Net Before You Invest

Before diving into investing, it is necessary to create an emergency fund. An emergency fund is money that you have saved in anticipation of dealing with unexpected expenses - such as a job loss, medical bills, car maintenance or last-minute travel. This safety net will allow you to weather every storm without having to sell your investments in a down market. Depending on the financial planner, the typical suggestion for an emergency fund is to save three to six months' worth of living expenses in a separate and easily accessible bank account. As an example, if your monthly expenses equal A\$4,000 - your emergency fund should be anywhere from A\$12,000 – A\$24,000.

Having this cushion will provide you peace of mind and financial stability to allow your investments to compound uninterrupted. It also provides you avoidance from spending on credit cards or taking out loans when life throws you a curveball. Think of this as your first step towards financial independency - a buffer of security so you can invest without worry.

Although there are many investing apps, I am using only two investing apps to invest in stock market in Australia and US. They are CommSec Pocket and Spaceship Voyager Apps. I find using these apps simple and easy to understand. In the next section, I provide step-by-step instructions to use the above-mentioned apps.

---

[8] ASX. *Australian Investor Study*, 2023.

Step-by-Step Instructions: How to Invest in the Australian Market Using CommSec Pocket

1. Go to Google play store and type CommSec pocket app and download the CommSec Pocket using the link CommSec Pocket - Apps on Google Play as given here.

2. Create an account in CommSec Pocket app. You might have to need to have a bank account with CommBank.
3. These are following ETFs available for investment in CommSec Pocket app. You can study each ETFs and buy the ETFs according to your available funds.

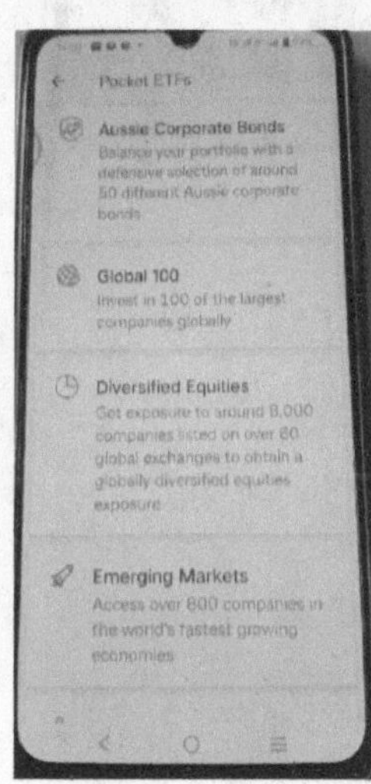

4. For example, you can buy Sustainability Leaders ETF, which provides exposure to diversified portfolios of global stocks which engage in environmentally friendly businesses. For this ETF, the minimum investment is 55 dollars. The minimum investment for each ETF varies.

5. Next, you can buy shares of Australian companies. There are around 2000 Australian shares listed on the Australian Stock Exchange (ASX) which can be bought through CommBank

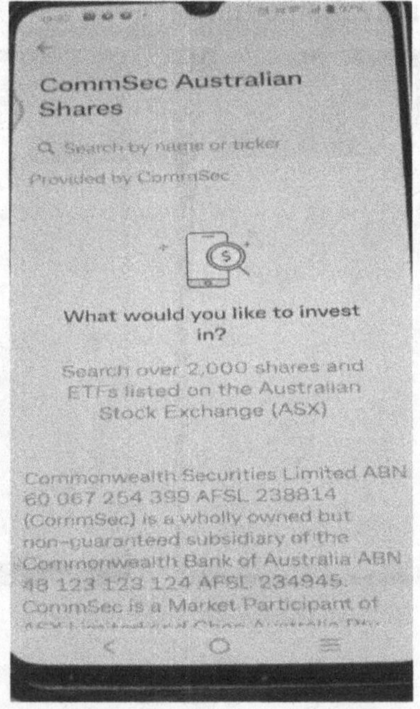

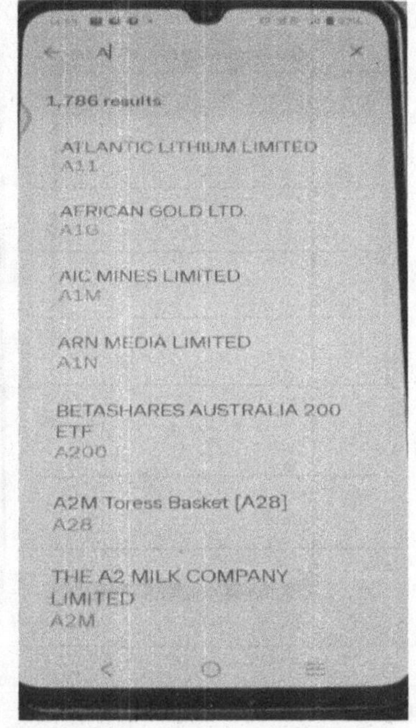

app. You can type first letter of company's name, and you will get list of companies starting with that letter.

When you invest for the first time in the any individual company shares in the Australian Stock Exchange, it must be at least for A$500. After this, you can invest in the same company shares for A$100 or more.

For example, if you want to buy shares of Coles company and we can type Coles, and we will get the following:

The market price of one share of Coles Group Limited is A$21.770. The max price in one year is A$23.960 and minimum price is A$17.770 and has increased by A$4 which is an increase of 22.51%. It also provides information about the latest dividend disbursed to shareholders as given below:

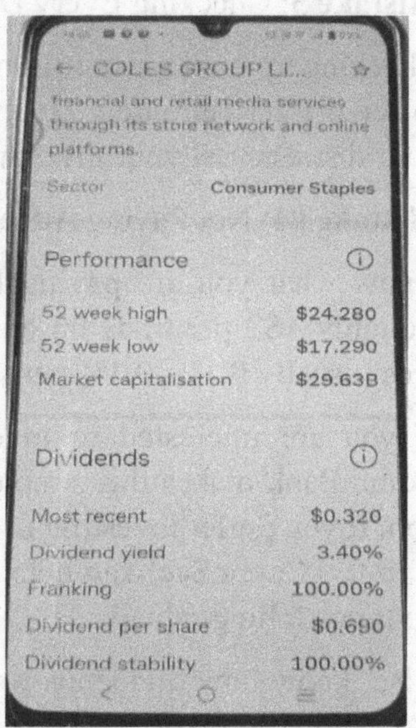

Common Beginner Mistakes and How to Avoid Them

Mistake #1 - Waiting For the Right Time

The biggest mistake is waiting for the 'right time' The right time to start was yesterday; the second-best time to start is today.

If you invest A$100 a month for ten years with an average of 8%, you will have just over A$18,000 but if you wait three years, it will only be A$13,000. That is A$5,000 you gave up just waiting to decide.

Mistake #2 - Investing Based on Fear of Missing Out

Never invest in a stock just because it has a lot of social media hype. Real investing is based on rigorous research, not hearsay.

If you cannot understand the company, then do not invest in it.

Mistake 3: Checking Every Day

Checking up on your portfolio every day is akin to digging up a seed to see if it has sprouted. This will not help you; it would only lead to your distress. Let your investments breath.

Mistake #4: Not Paying Attention to Taxes and Fees

Know what you are paying for. CommSec Pocket has a small fee (roughly A$2 per trade up to A$1,000) and ETFs have management fees (usually 0.1%–0.3% per year).

If you are interested in investing in shares in Australia directly, CommBank makes this simple for you through their mobile banking app. If you prefer investing in diversified ETFs, the CommSec Pocket App (by CommSec) can help you start with small amounts and build your portfolio gradually.

Also, know how dividends would be taxed and how franking credits works in your favor.

Ashfaq is a 27-year-old software engineer from Pakistan who moved to Sydney on a work visa and was always interested in investing but assumed it was 'too much'. One night, a friend showed him CommSec Pocket.

He started with A$200 in an Australian Dividend ETF and then contributed A$50 for each month.

After one year, he had accrued A$24 in dividends and the ETF had increased in value by roughly 6%. Most importantly, he became confident. He said, 'I realised it is not about how much money I spend; it is about building a habit. Once I saw how easy it was to understand the app and returns, I wanted to learn more.'

Ashfaq is now going to slowly diversify into US stocks but his base started right here in Australia.

Building a Smart, Tax-Aware Investment Plan

The secret to achieving success can be found in not trying to guess what the market will do fancy. The secret is aligning the plan with your goals and his unique situation.

1.   **Define Your Financial Goals**

You should be asking yourself the following:

Am I investing for short-term growth, or for long-term wealth?

Am I seeking ongoing passive income (dividends) or am I investing for gradual capital appreciation for the long term?

What degree of risk can I tolerate?

2.   **Define your portfolio balance**

A healthy portfolio might look something like this:

70% broad Australian exchange traded funds (ETFs)

20% dividend ETFs

10% individual shares that you understand

3. Consider taxes

The franking credit system in Australia rewards long-term investors.

As a residency, you will be able to claim credits for the company tax that has already been paid. As a temporary resident there may be investment types where you pay less tax - just always check your visa and tax status.

4. Stick with it

Even modest short-term investments, done continuously, will build momentum. The sage advises, 'Consistency is better than intensity.'

In recent years, Australia's inflation rate has averaged between 3 and 4% per year. This implies that your money is gradually losing value if it is sitting in a bank account doing nothing. Making your money work for you rather than allowing inflation to devalue it is crucial because something that costs A$100 today could cost A$103 or more the following year.

Australian stocks have historically produced high returns, averaging roughly 8.8% annually over the previous thirty years[9]. By contrast, the majority of savings accounts have only provided 2–3%. This disparity demonstrates why making even modest market investments can result in far higher long-term growth than merely saving money.

In the meantime, the growth of Exchange Traded Funds (ETFs) demonstrates how investing is now easier than ever. Since 2020, the number of Australians who own ETFs has increased by 45% to over 2.3 million[10]. Without requiring substantial sums of money or in-depth financial knowledge, these funds enable regular investors to own tiny shares of multinational corporations and industries.

Investing in the Australian market is not just about making money, it is about building confidence, control, and connection.

---

[9] Vanguard Australia. *Investment Returns Report*, 2024.
[10] ASX. *ETF Market Growth Report*, 2023.

It teaches you how the economy works, how businesses grow, and how to make your money work for you.

The ASX is not an obscure, complicated system, it is a living network of companies that directly impact your life every day.

The supermarket you shop at, the phone you use, the bank you save with, all part of that network.

And now, you can be part of that too.

When you invest at home, you are not just purchasing a share, you are purchasing freedom for your future.

Trading stocks

It refers to the purchase and sale of a company's share, listed on the stock market, in order to utilise fluctuations in the market. Investing focuses on long-term growth while trading concentrates on opportunities that occur over a shorter time frame. One of the biggest benefits of trading stocks is liquidity; you can purchase and sell shares rapidly as you require.

Trading also provides flexibility, as you can react to news or market price changes as they happen. Successful traders often maximize returns through the use of research, trend analysis, and timing. Another benefit, if timing is done properly, is capital growth; stock trading can yield higher profits than a traditional savings account or fixed deposit.

Nevertheless, trading requires discipline, patience, and an understanding of risk; best to start small, stay aware of what is happening in the market, and trade only in companies or ETFs you understand. Trading platforms like CommBank and CommSec, have made trading Australian shares safe and easy, even for beginners.

Self-Reflection Questions:

1. What fears or beliefs are the reasons that I have not invested locally yet?
2. At what amount can I realistically invest every month that will not cause financial stress?
3. What Australian company or industry do I already know and trust?
4. Am I committed to continuing if the market goes downward?

Chapter 4:
Expanding Horizons:
Investing in the US Stock Market
from Australia

For a long time, Australians have relied on their money being with local heavyweights, the big four banks, the mining sector, and property. It is all well-trodden ground for them. But recently there has been a quiet revolution under way. Thousands of Australians are now crossing borders with their investments, financially, not physically. They are purchasing shares in businesses such as Apple, Microsoft, Google, and Tesla without leaving their home.

Investing overseas once seemed daunting or out of reach because it requires brokers, paperwork, and a lot of money. Now, thanks to technology and platforms like Spaceship Voyager, Stake, and CommSec International, Australians have the option of owning part of some of the world's most cutting-edge businesses at the touch of their finger.

A recent Finder Investment Report for 2024 outlines that about 38% of Australian retail investors now own international shares, which was more than double from 2019[11]. This is because the US stock market uses the S&P 500 as an index, and has provided better returns than most other indices in the world, averaging returns of approximately 10% over the past 50 years[12]. By way of comparison, the ASX 200 has provided returns of about 7% for most of that period, which all adds up over time.

So, why is this important? Because investing internationally is not just an attempt to get better investment returns, it is about harnessing the growth of global economies. The companies that are going to shape our future, whether it be in AI, clean energy, or something else, are

---

[11] Finder Australia. *Global Investing Report*, 2024.
[12] S&P Dow Jones Indices. *Historical Annual Returns Data*, 2024.

usually started and establishing themselves in the US market. Investing internationally gives Australian investors that story as well.

When you think of your phone, laptop or streaming service, there is a high likelihood that it is an American company. These businesses are responsible for not just the United States market but the world market. Investing in these companies provides exposure back to the very trends that shape our everyday lives.

The 5 largest US market cap companies in 2025, with their TDB value (1 trillion is equivalent to 1,000 billion), Apple, Microsoft, Amazon, Alphabet - Google, and Nvidia, will be valued over A$13 trillion in value, or over half of the total GDP for the US. They have matched scale, innovation, benefit globally from systemic advantages, and that is why every investor wants exposure here.

In the past, you would have to navigate complicated trading paperwork to open a foreign brokerage account. However, investing internationally in American companies as an Australian has never been easier thanks to beginner app-based brokers like Spaceship Voyager or any other investing apps now.

With Spaceship Voyager, you can invest in professionally managed funds that contain a range of assets, notably shares of major global companies. You can make an investment starting from A$5 and the app automatically invests your dollar across dozens of US and international stocks.

Spaceship Voyager, CommSec pocket or any other investing app opens a world of investing for everyday people, granting direct access to over 6,000 US stocks and ETFs. You can buy fractional shares, so if someone wanted to own A$15 worth of Apple or Tesla, they can.

These tools have made investing globally accessible to everyone, challenging the old-wives-tale that you need to be wealthy to invest in global markets. For instance, 2023 ASX Investor Study found that 42% of new under 30 investors started with less than A$500, it is no longer about how much you can invest, but if you can contribute consistently.

Step-by-Step Instructions: Investing in the US Market Using Spaceship Voyager

1. Go to Google Play Store and download the spaceship voyager app Space Voyager - Apps on Google Play which looks like this:

2. Click on the blue button to join the spaceship. You might have to provide your passport and necessary identification documents to indicate that you are residents of Australia such as utility bills, student ID or bank card (numbers, pin should be hidden) and tax file number. This might take few days.

3. Here is a deal from me. There is an option to provide the referral code. Since I am user of this app, I can give you my referral code which is provided below: You can click on the website link provided below and provide your necessary personal details. You will receive A$30 if you enter the code *S8WUG8SV50*

within 14 days of signing up and investing a minimum of A$15 in your selected portfolio (provided in next step)within 90 days of opening the account.

Hey. Start investing with Spaceship Voyager today! Get A$30 in your account when you enter this code S8WUG8SV50 within 14 days of signing up and invest at least $15 in your chosen portfolio within 90 days of signing up. T&Cs apply. Spaceship Voyager issued by Spaceship Capital Ltd AFSL 501605. General advice only. Consider the PDS on our website before making a decision to invest with Spaceship Voyager. https://spaceship.onelink.me/FDhV/S8WUG8SV50

If you link on the above link, you will see this page given below:

Note: Please be informed that above Spaceship referral code is valid for 14 days from the date of opening your account/signing up. Please enter the referral code within 14 days and invest A$15 dollars within 90 days of signing

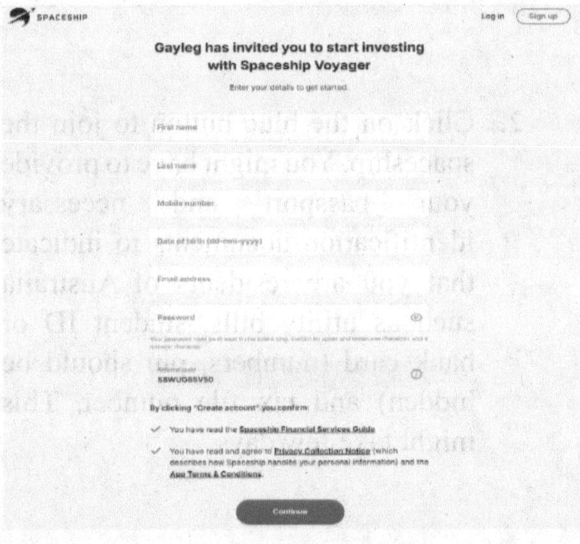

up. If you enter the referral code after the 14-day period, you will not receive the bonus.

4   You will fill in the details to open your account. There are five portfolios you can choose to invest A$15 to receive A$30 from the Spaceship Voyager App within 14 days of signing up. They

Invest in Australian and US Stock Market and Make Money

are Spaceship Galaxy Portfolio, Spaceship Explorer Portfolio, Spaceship Universe Portfolio, Spaceship Origin Portfolio and Spaceship Earth Portfolio.

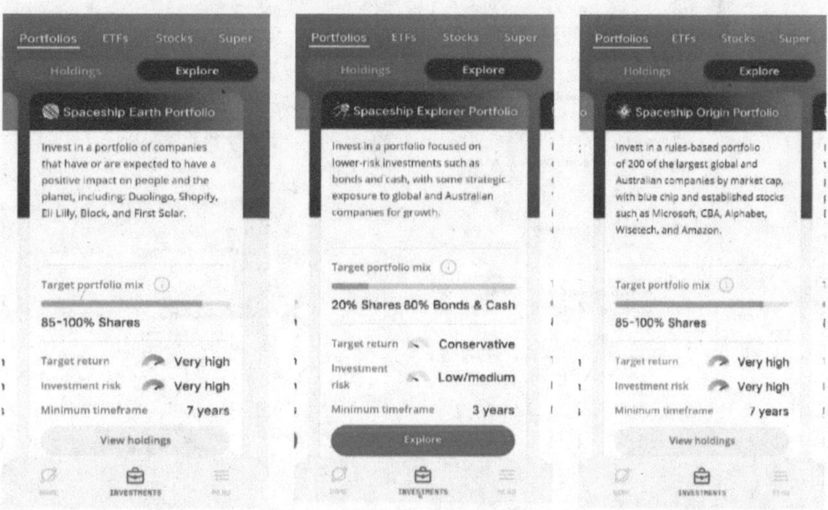

5   To invest in the United State stock market, there are two ways to do it. First, you can invest in ETFs which can give you an access to top 500 companies and other ETFs in the US. It is considered to be less risky than investing in individual companies' shares. Some of the ETFs in US Stock Market are given:

6   Next, you can also invest in shares of individual companies. For example, you can invest in your favourite companies (Microsoft, Google, Netflix, Tesla, etc.) as given below:

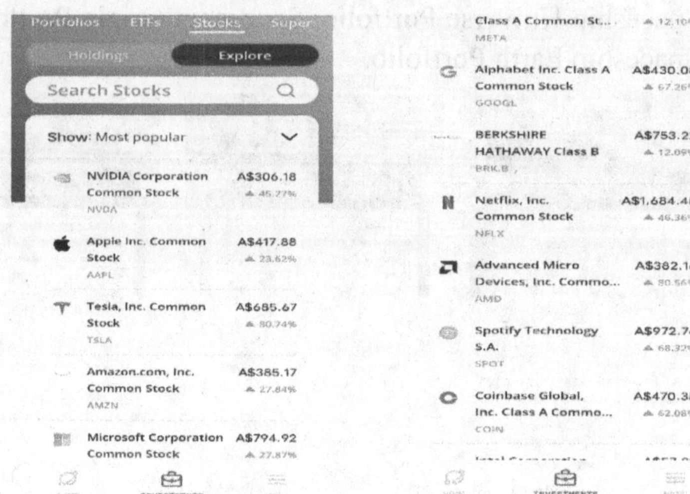

However, these shares can be volatile when compared to ETFs. Please be informed that you do not require huge amount of money to buy the above shares. The minimum investment amount is A$10.00.

Understanding the Risks and Rewards

Investing internationally allows for opportunity, but it also exposes you to additional risk. Let us break that down.

1. **Currency Risk** - If you are investing in the US, some or all of your return will be dependent on the AUD-USD exchange rate. For example, if the Australian dollar rises in value, your returns (in AUD) might decrease, or if the Australian dollar falls, your returns may increase somewhat. To put this into context, during 2020, when the AUD fell from $0.70 to $0.58 USD, Australian investors in US stocks enjoyed an extra 20 percent from the currency movement, without even counting market appreciation[13].

---

[13] Reserve Bank of Australia. *Exchange Rate Data*, 2020.

2. **Market Volatility** - US stocks can be very volatile, especially in the technology sector. It is important to take a long view. History tells us that the S&P 500 has made a full recovery after every major crash such as the ones in 2008 and again in 2020. Generally, long term investors who remained invested recovered their investments and made money thereafter.

3. **Taxation** - Residents of Australia are taxed on their worldwide investment income under the Foreign Income Tax Offset. This typically means, for example, you will pay US withholding tax on dividends (usually 15%) and receive a credit on your Australian tax return. This can be made easier through apps that automatically manage the process, like Stake or Spaceship.

Michael, 32, from Brisbane, began making an investment of $100 a week into US tech ETFs from 2022. In 2023, the USD weakened and the returns on the investment appeared much smaller in AUD returns. Consequently, he was frustrated by the international currency experience and thought about selling. Instead, he remained patient and did not sell.

In mid-2025, the value of his portfolio increased by 15% against the USD and, when there was a weaker AUD, the return in AUD was a remarkable 22%. Michael learned from his investment experience, that currency tends to balance itself out in time. Investing and maintaining a focus on some core fundamentals was the best decision.

Growth vs. Dividend Stocks, Finding Your Fit

Not all investors are looking for the same outcomes. Some are looking for growth, companies are reinvesting their profits to grow their companies very quickly. Others would prefer dividends, reliable wages in order to get some form of income.

Growth stocks (e.g., Tesla, Amazon, Nvidia) can surge quickly but fluctuate more.

Dividend stocks (e.g., Coca-Cola, Johnson & Johnson) offer reliable returns and passive income.

Of course, a combination will usually be the most effective path: maintain a core group of dividend payers for stability and invest in some growth stocks to increase your wealth over time.

Emma and Jake, both 28, started investing A$200 a month in 2020.

Emma chose growth ETFs like the NASDAQ 100.

Jake picked dividend ETFs focusing on companies with regular payouts.

By 2025, Emma's account balanced at A$28,350 (approximately a 10% annualised return) and Jake's account balance was A$24,750 while he earned A$600 per year in dividends. In both cases, each investor was successful, Emma had a higher value return and Jake received income on an ongoing basis.

The main message is: do what fits your style, and what your goals are. If a principal concern is stability and reliability, then choose dividend generating stocks. If making a lot in value is your goal, then you must be able to handle the mood swings of a volatile market, but the potential reward could be higher.

Diversification and Emotional Discipline

International investing is also a measure any investor can develop and define as emotional maturity in the investing world. The more diversifiable your portfolio may be - by countries, sectors and types of assets you own - the more effective it is at weathering shocks in its value.

Research by Vanguard (2024), diversified global portfolios can offset 25 % more volatility for their investors during times of market downturns[14]. So, in accordance with advice from seasoned investors: do not put all your eggs in one basket.

Emotional discipline is equally significant. During market declines, you may be tempted, through fear, to sell. But history has shown that patience will win. If you invested A$10,000 into the S&P 500 in 2000 and remained invested until 2025, and endured through the crashes of 2008 and 2020, your portfolio would now be worth over A$70,000. Those who sold in panic 'paid the price' typically earning a lot less.

Tools Available to Help You Remain Consistent

1. Spaceship Voyager – automatic investing, low fees, and simplified UX.
2. Stake – direct US stock trading with fractional shares.
3. CommSec International – for a more advanced investor seeking broader access to the market.
4. Super Funds & ETFs – many Australian superannuation funds now provide access to US exposure, enabling the simplest diversification.

These platforms enable you to learn at your own pace while viewing your portfolio and compounding your financial literacy gradually, and allowing you to form a habitual investing pattern rather than a one-time investment experience.

The compounding power globally: This capability is truly the greatest value of the global investment. A simple example is as follows: If you invested A$200 per month at a 9% average annual return, after twenty years you would have approximately A$131,000 – of which about A$83,000 would be compounded growth above any contributions.

This is why Australian's view an investment now as a habit, rather than a one-time investment decision. The compounding is no different from

---

[14] Vanguard. *Diversification and Risk Report*, 2024.

your approach to fitness or learning. Being consistent will compound your education or fitness results over time!

A Global Mindset, A Personal Mission

Entering the US market is not only a financial opportunity, but rather a mindset change. It is going beyond your comfort zone, having confidence in your knowledge, and allowing your money to work on your behalf toward a better world.

When you buy one share of Apple, you are investing in a company, yes, but more importantly, you are investing in innovation, creativity, and human potential. If you invested in Tesla, you are investing in the future and advocating for clean energy. Investing globally demonstrates a belief in the future that is greater than the future of one nation.

The most successful investors are not necessarily the smartest or do not make the best decisions rather they are the most business-like or consistent. They learn, they change, and they are patient. Now that you are in the position as an Australian investor, you have access to the world's strongest and dynamic market like never before, and this can usually be a positive access to wealth creation.

Start small, think big, and remember that financial independence is not built overnight. It is built step by step, decision after decision, and investment after investment.

Self-Reflection Questions

1. Which international companies motivate me, and do their principles correspond with my intentions in terms of investments?
2. How much volatility can I bear on a short-term basis for potential long-term gains?
3. What percentage of my paycheck could I comfortably invest every month?
4. What type of investor would I want to be in five years – conservative, balanced, or aggressive?

Chapter 5:
Mindset, Mistakes, and
the Road to Financial Freedom

Many individuals assume that becoming a successful investor has much to do with timing the market, picking the right stocks, or having a PhD in finance. In truth, it is not about the market at all; it is about the mindset. The best investors are not those who have a connection to the market that allows them to identify trends perfectly. The best investors are those who stay calm when the market shakes, consistent when they lose motivation, and are long-term focused when everyone else is looking for the next trend or shortcut to making money.

The market - Australian or American - rewards discipline and patience in investing, unlike the instant-everything we have grown accustomed to: quick profits, trends that go viral, account viewings by the day, deliveries the next day, etc. We are used to living in an instant-gratification society, when the reality of building wealth is usually slow, systematic, and sometimes dull.

A 2024 Vanguard Investor Behaviour Study indicated that an average investor who remained invested in diversified ETFs for 10 years earned an average return of 8.1% annually, while a fleet of other investors who were in and out of investments more frequently earned only 4.2% on average annually[15]. The expectation gap was not about who knew more; it was about emotional discipline.

This chapter is about that discipline - doing the work on the inside to create wealth on the outside.

---

[15] Vanguard. *Investor Behaviour Study*, 2024.

Patience Over Profits, The Long Game of Real Investing

When you sow a seed, you do not dig it up each week to check on its progress. You water it, and provide it with some affection, and let time do the rest. Investing is similar to this.

Most novice investors lose money not so much because the investments were bad, but because they were not patient enough to let good investments time to develop. Once investors start receiving dividends, the temptation to either 'cash out' with a small profit or panic and sell when the price drops will undermine compounding and limit or eliminate the growth of real wealth.

According to the 2023 ASX Investor Report, almost 37% of new investors sold their initial shares before the six-month mark. Those unplanned exits prevented their investments from achieving long-term growth, while their portfolios could have increased in value by up to threefold in three years. Those who remained through volatility earned 42% higher returns than those who sold.

The message is simple: the market rewards patience, not the ability to predict the future.

Amelia, a 29-year-old nurse from Melbourne, started investing in 2018 with CommSec Pocket, investing A$50 a month. During the 2020 COVID-19 market crash, her A$2,000 portfolio dropped to approximately A$1,100. Most of her friends sold without thinking or fear, but Amelia did not. She adhered to her '5-year rule,' vowing to herself not to assess an investment until it had developed for at least 5 years.

By 2023, her investment had recovered to A$3,400, a 70% gain over her initial capital. Today, she continues to put money away every month. Her secret? She knew that wealth develops through years, not weeks.

This is not a luck story; it is about believing in the process. The market challenged her patience, but patience, in turn, became profit.

The Emotional Investor, Fear and Greed

We all experience the dual emotional adversities of fear and greed whilst investing.

Fear will make one sell when prices decrease.

Greed will entice one to chase the hot trend as everyone else is buying.

The trouble with both of these weaknesses is that they are emotional, not logical.

In 2021, for example, we witnessed a frenzy as retail investors piled into speculative stocks (GameStop, AMC, etc.) that social media made seem like a surefire way to make overnight wealth. When the movement fizzled, prices were down by over 80%. Many lost their life savings not due to bad luck, but because they responded to emotion rather than strategy.

This phenomenon is referred to as 'behavioural risk' by professional investors. The Morningstar Mind the Gap Report (2024) reported that investors underperform their own funds by an average of 1.7 % per annum simply because they buy high and sell low due to emotional triggers. Instead of trying to time the market, training your emotions is the best strategy.

The Growth Mindset, Learn Before You Earn

In investing, ignorance is costly. The difference between a fearful, emotional investor and a confident one is education.

Investors who understand how markets work, inflation, compounding, and diversifying make better choices even when misfortune strikes. The great thing about the digital age is that we can learn through apps, podcasts, and financial education platforms.

In a survey conducted by Finder Australia (2024), 61% of first-time investors who had taken at least one financial education course achieved higher returns than those who had not. The most significant difference was that the educated investors avoided emotional errors and chose a diversified portfolio.

In investing, learning is the new earning. Before one chases profit, let one build knowledge. Knowledge will better protect your money than any market forecast can.

Ethan, a 24-year-old international student studying in Perth, entered the market in 2021 after watching a YouTube video on how to 'get rich quickly from stocks.' Without doing any research, he started buying trending shares in electric vehicle startups. Before long, he lost A$700, half of his savings.

While most people would give up at that point, Ethan resolved to educate himself. He started with low-level investment books, began following Australian financial blogs, and began listening to podcasts such as The Australian Finance Podcast. He transitioned to investing in low-fee ETFs, began contributing to his portfolio monthly, and appropriately diversified his portfolio.

By 2025, Ethan's new portfolio was generating an average annual growth rate of 9%. His loss became a lesson learned and stated, 'Once I began treating investing like a skill rather than a shortcut, I stopped losing money.'

Avoiding Common Beginner Mistakes

When you first start investing, it is easy to get caught up in either excitement or fear, both of which can lead to costly mistakes. According to the ASX Investor Study (2023), it found that 'almost 42% of new investors indicated having made at least one major mistake (i.e. by buying or selling too quickly)' in their first year of investing. The benefit is that you can use any mistake to your advantage if you can grasp what mistakes you should avoid early in your investing career.

One of the most common 'traps' that you should be aware of is trying to time the market. Many new investors will wait for the right 'timing to buy or sell an investment. Even professionals with many years of experience are still trying to time market movements correctly.

Market volatility is common, and history shows that you are more often than not better off simply staying invested than trying to time market movements. For example, a Vanguard study (2024) found that investors who remained fully invested in the Australian share market from 2014 to 2024 earned an average annual return of 8.3%, while investors who missed the 10 best-performing days earned an average annual return of only 5.1%. In summary, focus on time IN the market, not timing OF the market.

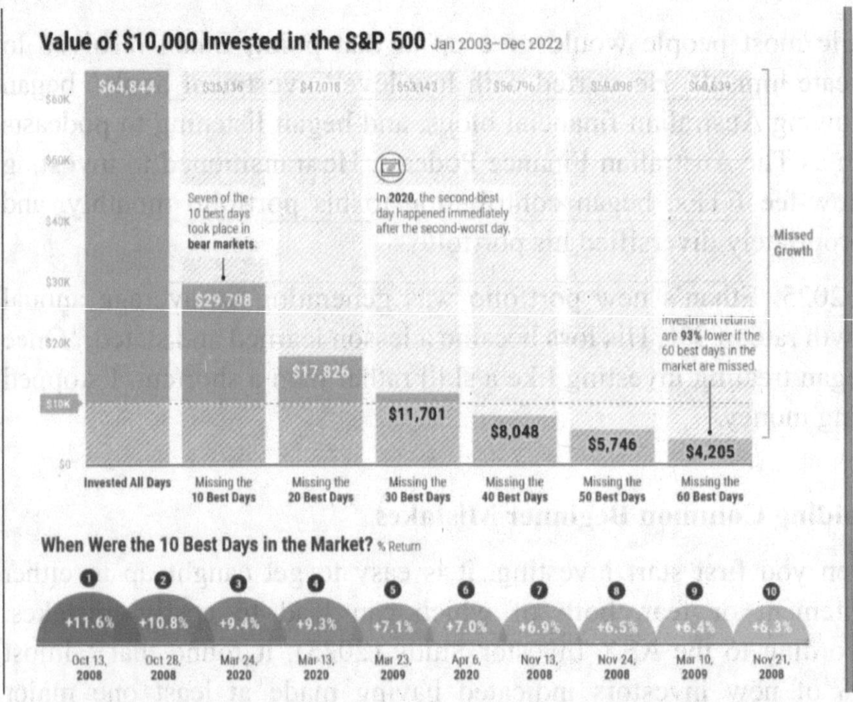

Attitudes toward investment risk by age group in Australia, ASX Australian Investor Study 2023.

Another common mistake is investing without clear goals. Another frequent misconception is to invest without a specific objective in mind. If you have not defined a particular reason for investing, be it to achieve financial independence, a house deposit, or retirement, every decline in the market seems like a personal affront.

Research shows investors with written goals are 30% more likely to remain consistent in a down market (finder.com.au Investment Report, 2024). Goals help you anchor your decisions and frame short-term volatility as temporary noise rather than a reason to panic.

Equally critical is to do your due diligence in diversifying, or putting your money in different assets rather than betting your whole investment on a company or industry. A well-balanced portfolio reduces exposure to significant losses and makes you a more stable long-term investor.

For example, in early 2022, those who held only tech shares saw declines of over 30%, while those with diversified investments saw declines of only a fraction of that. Exchange-traded funds (ETFs) provide an excellent way for beginners to diversify their assets with little effort.

Keep the small costs and comparisons in mind as well. Fees that you cannot see, paying fees for the platform or having bad tax management can slowly chip away at your gains over time; just a 1% fee could mean almost a 20% decrease in your total returns over 30 years (Morningstar Research, 2024[16]). Similarly, start comparing your progress to others, and you will invite more frustration than necessary. Each of us has our own timeline, income and goals, so there is no accurate measure for you other than your own consistency.

Mistakes will be made, but if you learn from them early on, they will help you become a more informed and confident investor over time. Money underneath it all is not the goal; it is freedom: freedom to work when you want, spend time with family and friends, travel, or just live 'normally' without worrying about money. That is the real return we receive on investing. In the NAB 2023 Wealth Report, Australians who were consistent in investing even small amounts reported 29% more

---

[16] Morningstar. *Impact of Fees on Long-Term Investment Returns*, 2024.

life satisfaction and 41% less financial stress compared to those who relied solely on savings[17].

Earning a high income is one thing; being in control of your life is another.

Financial independence rests on three principles:

Knowledge - knowing how money works.

Consistency - investing regularly, regardless of the amount.

Mindset - remaining calm and collected through uncertainty.

The journey to wealth is more about the emotions than the numbers.

Take Jacob and Lily, a married couple from Adelaide. They approached money very differently. Jacob was a saver and Lily a believer in investing. After much coaxing in 2019, Lily had her husband, Jacob, invest A$250 a month into ETFs with Spaceship Voyager, while Jacob left his money in a savings account.

Fast forward to 2025. Lily had invested A$18,000 and was sitting on about A$26,900. Jacob had A$19,300 in his savings account, just above the amount he deposited after inflation. The turning point was realising that Lily's money was doing more than just making the family more money almost effortlessly; it was about freedom. The returns on their investment were passive enough that they could take short trips without disrupting their emergency reserve.

Shortly afterwards, Jacob began participating, automatically contributing money to his own investments. Today, they would both describe money and investing as exciting life events rather than stressful obligations. For them, investing was not a financial obligation; it was a joint mission.

---

[17] National Australia Bank (NAB). *Wealth and Wellbeing Report*, 2023.

Discipline and Consistency: The Silent Superpower

The most significant distinction between people who create wealth and those who do not will not be their intelligence; it will be their habits.

For example:

What if you invested A$150/month at an 8% return?

In five years: A$10,900

In ten years: A$27,900

In twenty years: A$74,500

See, that is what consistency can get you.

Not once or twice a year, but every single month, like brushing your teeth.

Tiny, consistent actions bountifully accumulate into significant results. Consistency also looks like sticking to your system.

This was precisely what Investor Warren Buffett said, 'The stock market is a mechanism for transferring money from the impatient to the patient.'

How to Build an Investor's Mindset

Here are five mental models to help keep you grounded:

1. Think Long Term: If you would not hold a company for 10 years, do not hold it for 10 minutes.
2. Detach emotion. Focus on value rather than attention-grabbing headlines.
3. Automate your investments. Remove decision fatigue.
4. Celebrate the times when you do not panic sell. Every time you do that, you just get stronger.
5. Track your progress annually, not daily. Very rarely are people going to panic on annual returns; we will on a daily price.

The market goes up and down, but over time, compounding is proportional to that length of time.

When you hold this mindset, you become trained to act from intention rather than pressure.

Priya is a 27-year-old accounting student at Sydney who set herself the challenge of investing for 75 days. Each day, she learned one new thing about finance, whether a podcast, an article, or a video and made a A$10 weekly investment through Spaceship Voyager app. After 75 days, she did not just have a portfolio; she gained confidence. Her habit of spending A$100 turned into A$3,000 by the end of the year. More importantly, she noted, 'I stopped being fearful of money. I started being in control of it.' Her story shows us that freedom is not just financial; it is mental.

The road to financial freedom is not strict. It is more like a road with lessons, small wins, setbacks, and personal growth. But that destination is worth every step forward.

At this point, you have learned the logic, tools, and psychology of investing, from starting with small investments on the ASX, to global stocks, and learning how to manage your own emotional discipline of investing. But the last step is action.

Financial freedom does not begin with wealth; it starts with intent.

Every dollar we invest with intent becomes a vote for our future, a vote to say, 'I choose growth over fear, I choose learning over luck, and I choose patience over panic.'

The Path Towards Your Financial Freedom Starts Here.

The first time you ever held this book, you may have had a moment of doubt - not knowing where to start, unsure if investing is worthwhile, intimidated by financial jargon, or presumed investing is only for 'rich' or 'experienced' people. As you learned in each chapter, it is not that complicated: financial freedom is not about luck. Economic freedom is about cultivating a mindset, learning, knowledge, and taking small steps consistently.

In a society where money seems to account for most of our stress, one of the most empowering things you can do is learn how to make money work for you. You can be a student, a young professional, or someone getting a late start. The moment you decide to take control of your finances, you are taking control of your future.

Through this book, you have learned the basics of investing, from the Australian Stock Exchange (ASX) to international markets such as the United States (US). You have seen how regular people with regular incomes-built wealth solely through consistency, patience, and a long-term mindset.

You learned how to open your first investment account in CommSec Pocket or Spaceship Voyager apps, discover ETFs, dividends, and how these investments could lead to streams of passive income.

You also learned about the emotional and psychological side of investing, why people are fearful when markets drop, and how consistency trumps intelligence over the long term.

Most importantly, you have learned that the ultimate goal of investing is not money; the real goal is freedom, freedom to make choices, freedom to do work you love, freedom not to worry, freedom to support those you love and to take control of the life you live, according to the values and dreams you have.

From Scarcity to Abundance

If you have ever thought, 'I do not have enough to get started investing,' remember: every successful investor has believed to the same way. They started with A$10, A$50, or A$100, not thousands of dollars. What mattered is not how much, but that they made that first commitment and stayed consistent.

In Australia, recent studies show that 37 per cent of millennials now invest regularly - a huge jump from 8 years ago, when only 18 per cent did. Investors who took advantage of compounding returns and invested early, even with small amounts, are already experiencing its value. This is the beauty of time in the market - allowing your money to work quietly while you live your life.

The fact is, the earlier you start investing, the easier it becomes; but even if you have not started at an earlier life stage, it is never too late. The market does not pay you for being perfect; it rewards you for showing up!

The Mindset That Sustains Success

By this point, you may have figured out that investing is less about figures, and more about behaviour. It is not about forecasting the market, it is about priming your mindset. It is this trait that links all successful investors, from Warren Buffett to the average Australian downloading investment apps like CommSec Pocket or Spaceship Voyager app.

Successful investors do not chase every market move. Successful investors do not panic when the market goes down. Successful investors remain calm, stick to their plan and let time do all the work!

This is what differentiates *trading* from *investing*.

Real wealth creation happens when you treat investing like a habit, not a hobby. Just like exercise, or healthy eating, the results will be slow at first, and then become successful! With every automatic transfer to your investment account, and every new piece of knowledge and patience in your decisions, you will start to compound into real, lasting wealth

Investing involves not only numbers but also psychology. The hardest part is not choosing the appropriate stock but managing your feelings when the market reaches new highs and new lows. Most investors unconsciously go through the same emotional cycle. You can see the cycle below: it begins with optimism and euphoria as the market rises, and it ends with fear and panic as the market declines. Acknowledging this response may help keep you grounded as others act irrationally[18].

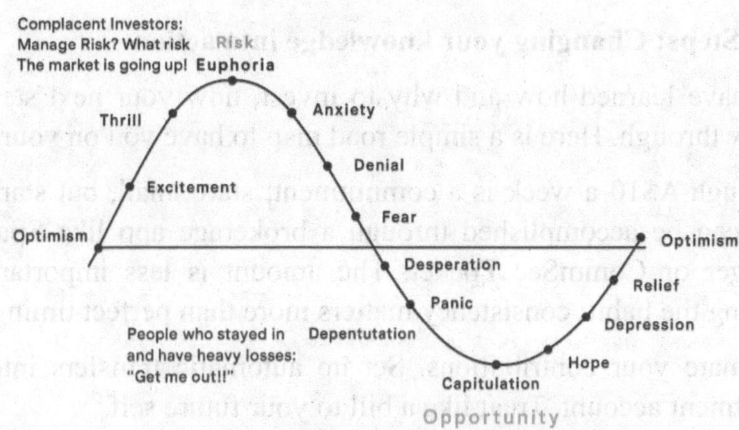

The emotional cycle of investing, ASX / Betashares

Redefining Wealth

Most people think that wealth is cars, houses, and luxury but mostly true wealth, is pretty simple. It is peace and freedom. It is about being able to wake up and trust that any emergency will not destroy everything you have built. It is choosing to work because you want, not because you have to!

Your investment portfolio is not just a collection of assets on your phone; it is a portfolio of potential options for a life of freedom! Each stock purchased and every dollar saved grow your freedom fund in preparation for a future on your terms.

---

[18] Betashares. (2023). *Four emotions that can affect your investment decisions.* Retrieved from https://www.betashares.com.au/insights/four-emotions-that-can-affect-your-investment-decisions/

And remember, wealth is how you elevate your life. It allows you to give back to your family, help your community, or contribute to the movements and causes you care about. That is the nature of abundance, with giving, abundance continues to grow.

Next Steps: Changing your knowledge into action

You have learned how and why to invest, now your next step is to follow through. Here is a simple road map to have you on your path:

Although A$10 a week is a commitment; start small, but start now! This can be accomplished through a brokerage app like Spaceship Voyager or CommSec Pocket. The amount is less important than creating the habit; consistency matters more than perfect timing.

Automate your contributions. Set up automatic transfers into your investment account. Treat like a bill to your future self.

Look back at your goals every 6–12 months. Are you aligned with your investments? Adapt, rebalance, and learn as you go.

Keep learning; read credible finance blogs and/or Australian YouTube educators or podcasts. The more you learn and consume information; the more you can elevate your investment skill set and be confident.

Do not compare your journey. Everyone will start from a different place. Focus on progress, not perfection.

Think seriously and long - ignore short-term noise. Allow compounding to work its quiet magic over time, not just weeks.

A Final Word: Your Financial Freedom Awaits

You do not have to be rich, brilliant, or lucky to be free. You just have to start.

Every chapter in this book has shown you everyday people - students, immigrants, young families, build extraordinary futures based on simple practices taken consistently over time. They did not wait until the time was right; they made time work for them.

Now it is your turn. Start today - wherever you are at. Because every dollar you invest today is not a dollar saved, it is a vote for your future self.

Years from now, you will not remember the ups and downs of the market - you will remember the day you took your control back.

Let that day be today. Your journey toward financial independence has begun, and it starts today. It starts with the courage to believe in your potential.

You are your best investment.

Self-Reflection Questions

1. What thoughts and feelings emerge when markets rise or fall and how do they influence my choices?
2. Specifically, am I investing in a manner that seeks outsized returns on a short timeframe or am I investing for long-term autonomy?
3. What behavioral habits or attitudes about money do I need to 'unlearn' so that I can develop gold standard investor behavior?
4. In ten years, how would I like my investments to influence my lifestyle and peace of mind?